0 Risk Startup-Business

Lesson On Wealth With Complete Entrepreneur Zero Risk Guide To Build Billionaire Mindset

Andrew B. Williams

**Copyright © by Andrew B. Williams 2024.
All rights reserved.**

Before this document is duplicated or reproduced in any manner, the publisher's consent must be gained. Therefore, the contents within can neither be stored electronically, transferred, nor kept in a database. Neither in Part nor full can the document be copied, scanned, faxed, or retained without approval from the publisher or creator.

Table Of Contents

INTRODUCTION

Chapter 1
Understanding Risk
Understanding Your Risk Tolerance
Assessing Your Business Idea's Risk

Chapter 2
Building a Strong Foundation
Building a Strong Online Presence and Website
Establishing a Customer Service and Support System

Chapter 3
Reducing Financial Risk
Managing Cash Flow and Finances
Managing Marketing and Sales Risk through Digital Channels

Chapter 4
Launch and Growth
Scaling Your Business for Success
Outsourcing and Automation Strategies

CONCLUSION

INTRODUCTION

Isabella was tired of the monotonous routine of her 9 to 5 job. She longed for something more, something that would spark her passion and creativity. So, she decided to take a leap of faith and start her own business.

After researching online, Isabella stumbled upon a book called 0 Risk Startup-Business Online. Intrigued by the title, she immediately purchased it and dived into its pages.

As she read through the book, Isabella was amazed by the insightful tips and strategies it provided. She learned about the importance of market research, creating a strong online presence, and building relationships with customers. She also discovered the value of taking calculated risks and embracing failure as a learning opportunity.

Armed with this newfound knowledge, Isabella began to put the book's teachings into practice. She conducted thorough market research to identify a niche that she was passionate about. She then created a website and social media profiles to showcase her products.

As Isabella launched her business online, she encountered challenges and setbacks along the way. But instead of giving up, she persevered and adapted her strategies based on the insights she gained from the book.

Months passed, and Isabella's business began to thrive. Customers were drawn to her authentic brand and quality products. She found fulfillment and joy in her work, knowing that she was following her passion and making a difference in the world.

Looking back, Isabella realized that buying the book 0 Risk Startup-Business Online was one of the best decisions she had ever made. It had not only equipped her with the knowledge and tools to succeed but also inspired her to dream big and pursue her entrepreneurial goals. And for that, she was forever grateful.

Chapter 1

Understanding Risk

Understanding Your Risk Tolerance

Risk tolerance is a crucial factor to consider when starting a 0-risk business. While the concept of a 0-risk business may sound appealing, it is important to remember that every business venture carries some level of risk. Understanding your risk tolerance is essential for making informed decisions and navigating the uncertainties that come with entrepreneurship.

One way to assess your risk tolerance in a 0-risk startup business is to evaluate your attitude towards risk and your capacity to handle losses. Are you okay with uncertainty and the possibility of failure? Do you have the financial resources to absorb potential losses without jeopardizing your financial stability? These are important questions to consider when determining your risk tolerance.

It is also important to be realistic about the potential risks involved in a 0-risk startup.

While the business may not involve financial investments or significant capital, there are other risks to consider, such as market demand, competition, and potential regulatory challenges. Understanding these risks and having a plan in place to mitigate them can help you make more informed decisions and better manage uncertainties.

Ultimately, understanding your risk tolerance in a 0-risk startup business is about knowing yourself and being honest about your capabilities and limitations. By being aware of your risk tolerance, you can make better decisions, set realistic expectations, and position yourself for success in your entrepreneurial journey.

Assessing Your Business Idea's Risk

Starting a business always involves some level of risk, no matter how well thought out your idea may be. However, there are ways to assess and mitigate this risk to increase your chances of success. In a "0 Risk" startup-business, it is important to carefully evaluate the potential risks associated with your business idea before moving forward. Here are some steps to help you assess the risk of your business idea:

1. **Market Research**: Conduct thorough market research to determine the demand for your product or service. Identify your target market and competitors to evaluate the competition and potential market size.

2. **Financial Analysis**: Create a detailed financial plan that outlines your startup costs, projected revenue, and potential return on investment. Consider factors such as pricing, sales forecasts, and cash flow projections.

3. **SWOT Analysis:** Conduct a SWOT analysis (strengths, weaknesses, opportunities, threats) to identify the internal and external factors that could impact your business. This will help you determine areas where you may be vulnerable and how to capitalize on opportunities.

4. **Legal and Regulatory Considerations**: Research any legal and regulatory requirements that may affect your business, such as licensing, permits, or industry regulations. Failure to comply with these requirements could pose a significant risk to your business.

5. **Risk Assessment**: Identify and evaluate potential risks that could impact your business, such as economic downturns, changing market conditions, or supply chain disruptions. Develop a risk management plan to mitigate these risks and develop contingency plans for potential challenges.

6. **Validate Your Idea:** Test your business idea with potential customers through surveys, focus groups, or beta testing. This will help you gather feedback and validate the demand for your product or service before investing significant time and resources.

By thoroughly assessing the potential risks associated with your business idea, you can make informed decisions and take steps to minimize the likelihood of failure. While it may not be possible to eliminate all risk entirely, being proactive and prepared can help you navigate challenges and increase your chances of success in your startup-business.

Chapter 2

Building a Strong Foundation

Building a Strong Online Presence and Website

Building a strong online presence and website is essential for any startup business looking to succeed in today's digital age. Having a well-designed website that accurately represents your brand and offerings can help attract customers and drive sales. Here are some tips on how to build a strong online presence and website for your startup business without taking on any unnecessary risks:

1. **Define your brand and target audience**: Before creating your website, it's important to define your brand identity and target audience. This will help you determine the design, messaging, and overall tone of your website.

2. **Choose the right platform**: There are plenty of website-building platforms available that cater to different needs and budgets. Choose one that offers the features and flexibility you need for your startup business.

3. **Optimize for search engines**: Make sure your website is optimized for search engines by using relevant keywords, meta tags, and high-quality content. This will help you improve your website's visibility and attract more organic traffic.

4. **Invest in quality content**: Content is king when it comes to building a strong online presence. Invest in creating high-quality, engaging content that resonates with your target audience and showcases your products or services.

5. **Utilize social media**: Don't underestimate the power of social media in building an online presence. Create profiles on popular platforms like Facebook, Instagram, and Twitter, and regularly engage with your audience to build brand awareness.

6. **Monitor and analyze performance**: Once your website is live, make sure to monitor its performance regularly using analytics tools. This will help you track visitor behavior, identify areas for improvement, and make data-driven decisions to optimize your online presence.

Establishing a Customer Service and Support System

Establishing a customer service and support system is essential for any startup business looking to build strong relationships with customers and drive satisfaction and loyalty. Here are some ways you can set up a customer service and support system for your startup business without taking on unnecessary risks:

1. **Choose the right communication channels**: Determine the communication channels that are most suitable for your customers, such as phone, email, live chat, social media, or self-service options. Consider the preferences and needs of your target audience when selecting the appropriate channels for providing customer support.

2. **Provide comprehensive training**: Invest in training for your customer service team to ensure they have the knowledge and skills needed to provide effective support to customers. Teach them how to handle inquiries, resolve issues, and maintain a positive attitude when interacting with customers.

3. **Implement a customer relationship management (CRM) system:** Use a CRM system to store customer information, track interactions, and manage relationships effectively.
A CRM system can help you streamline customer service processes, improve response times, and personalize interactions with customers.

4. **Monitor customer feedback**: Regularly collect and analyze customer feedback through surveys, reviews, and social media monitoring to identify areas for improvement and gauge customer satisfaction. Use this feedback to make data-driven decisions and enhance your customer service and support efforts.

5. **Offer personalized support:** Tailor your customer service and support approach to each customer's unique needs and preferences. Personalize interactions, provide relevant information, and demonstrate empathy and understanding to build trust and rapport with customers.

6. **Prioritize response times**: Aim to respond to customer inquiries and issues promptly to demonstrate your commitment to excellent customer service. Set clear response time goals and ensure that your customer service team is equipped to provide timely and efficient support.

Chapter 3

Reducing Financial Risk

Managing Cash Flow and Finances

Managing cash flow and finances effectively is crucial for the success and sustainability of any startup business. Here are some ways you can manage cash flow and finances in your startup business without taking on unnecessary risks:

1. **Create a budget**: Establish a budget that outlines your projected revenue, expenses, and cash flow for your startup business. Monitor your financial performance regularly and adjust your budget as needed to stay on track and avoid cash flow shortages.

2. **Monitor and track expenses:** Keep a close eye on your expenses and track them regularly to identify areas where you can cut costs and improve profitability.

Prioritize essential expenses and avoid unnecessary spending to preserve cash flow.

3. **Build a cash reserve:** Set aside a cash reserve to cover unexpected expenses or emergencies that may arise in your startup business.
Having a buffer can help you weather financial challenges and maintain stability in times of uncertainty.

4. **Negotiate favorable terms with suppliers and vendors**: Negotiate payment terms with your suppliers and vendors to optimize cash flow and improve your financial position. Explore discounts, early payment incentives, and flexible payment options to stretch your working capital.

5. **Invoice promptly and follow up on payments:** Invoice your customers promptly and follow up on payments to ensure timely receipt of funds. Implement clear payment terms, send reminders for overdue invoices, and establish a collections process to improve cash flow and reduce outstanding debts.

6. **Consider financing options**: Explore financing options, such as small business loans, lines of credit, or crowdfunding, to access additional capital for your startup business. Evaluate the costs and benefits of

different financing sources to determine the best fit for your financial needs.

7. **Invest in financial management tools:** Use financial management tools, such as accounting software, budgeting apps, and cash flow forecasting tools, to streamline your financial processes and gain insights into your business performance. Leverage technology to track expenses, manage invoices, and make informed financial decisions.

By implementing these strategies to manage cash flow and finances in your startup business, you can maintain financial stability, optimize resources, and position your business for long-term success. Prioritize financial planning, budget oversight, and proactive cash flow management to mitigate risks and ensure the financial health of your startup business.

Managing Marketing and Sales Risk through Digital Channels

When starting a new business, managing marketing and sales risks is crucial to ensure the success and sustainability of the venture. Leveraging digital channels is a cost-effective and efficient way to reach a large audience while minimizing risks. Here are some strategies for managing marketing and sales risks through digital channels in a 0 Risk Startup-Business:

1. **Targeted digital advertising**: Utilize targeted digital advertising platforms such as Google Ads, Facebook Ads, or LinkedIn Ads to reach potential customers who are already interested in your products or services. By focusing your marketing efforts on specific demographics, interests, and behaviors, you can maximize the impact of your advertising budget and minimize the risk of reaching irrelevant audiences.

2. **Content marketing**: Create valuable and engaging content such as blog posts, videos, or infographics that

provide helpful information to your target audience. Content marketing can help position your startup as an industry expert, build trust with potential customers, and drive organic traffic to your website through search engine optimization (SEO).

3. **Email marketing**: Build an email list of interested prospects and customers and send targeted and personalized email campaigns to nurture leads, promote new products or services, and drive sales. Email marketing is a cost-effective way to reach a captive audience and can be automated to save time and effort.

4. **Social media engagement**: Engage with your audience on social media channels such as Facebook, Twitter, Instagram, and LinkedIn to build relationships, gather feedback, and promote your brand. Social media platforms provide valuable insights into customer preferences and behaviors, allowing you to tailor your marketing and sales efforts to meet their needs.

5. **Customer relationship management (CRM)**: Implement a CRM system to manage and analyze customer interactions and data throughout the customer lifecycle. A CRM system can help track leads, manage sales opportunities, and provide valuable insights into customer behavior, preferences, and feedback.

6. **A/B testing and data analysis:** Continuously monitor and analyze the performance of your digital marketing and sales efforts through A/B testing, tracking key performance indicators (KPIs), and leveraging data analytics tools.

By testing different strategies, measuring results, and optimizing campaigns based on data-driven insights, you can identify areas for improvement and adjust your approach to maximize ROI.

Chapter 4

Launch and Growth

Scaling Your Business for Success

Scaling your business for success is a critical step in the growth and sustainability of your startup. While scaling involves inherent risks, there are strategies you can implement to manage and minimize these risks in a 0 Risk Startup-Business. Here are some tips for scaling your business effectively without taking on unnecessary risks:

1. **Focus on profitability**: Before scaling your business, ensure that your startup is generating consistent revenue and has a solid financial foundation. Focus on maximizing profitability through cost optimization, pricing strategies, and revenue growth before expanding operations.

2. **Streamline processes and operations**: To prepare your business for growth, streamline your processes and operations to increase efficiency and productivity. Identify bottlenecks, automate repetitive tasks, and standardize workflows to scale your business without sacrificing quality.

3. **Invest in technology and infrastructure:** Leverage technology to support your scaling efforts by implementing scalable systems, software, and tools that can accommodate increased demand and complexity. Invest in infrastructure upgrades and IT solutions to support growth and enhance operational capabilities.

4. **Develop a growth strategy**: Create a comprehensive growth strategy that outlines your goals, target market, competitive analysis, marketing and sales tactics, and operational plan for scaling your business.

5. **Expand your customer base:** Focus on expanding your customer base by reaching new markets, acquiring new customers, and retaining existing ones. Develop targeted marketing campaigns, offer promotions or discounts, and provide exceptional customer service to attract and retain loyal customers.

6. **Build a strong team**: As you scale your business, invest in building a strong team that can support growth and adapt to changing needs. Hire talented individuals,

provide training and development opportunities, and empower employees to contribute to the success of the business.

7. **Monitor and measure performance**: Continuously monitor and measure the performance of your scaled operations by tracking key performance indicators (KPIs), analyzing data, and making data-driven decisions. Regularly evaluate the success of your growth strategies and adjust course as needed to stay on track.

Outsourcing and Automation Strategies

Outsourcing Strategies:

1. **Identify non-core functions**: Determine which aspects of your business operations are non-core or time-consuming tasks that can be outsourced to third-party providers. These may include administrative tasks, customer support, accounting, or marketing services.

2.**Partner with specialized vendors**: Find reputable vendors or service providers who specialize in the areas you wish to outsource. Conduct thorough research, check references, and establish clear expectations and communication channels to ensure a successful partnership.

3. **Leverage freelancers or remote workers**: Utilize the flexibility of hiring freelancers or remote workers to fulfill specific tasks or projects on-demand. Platforms like Upwork, Fiverr, and Freelancer offer access to a wide pool of talent across various industries.

4. **Focus on scalability and cost-effectiveness**: Outsourcing allows you to scale your operations quickly and cost-effectively without the overhead costs associated with hiring full-time employees.
Evaluate the cost-benefit ratio of outsourcing versus in-house operations to determine the most efficient approach.

Automation Strategies:
1. **Identify repetitive tasks**: Identify repetitive or manual tasks within your business processes that can be automated to increase efficiency and productivity. Examples include data entry, email marketing, inventory management, and customer service inquiries.

2. **Implement workflow automation tools**: Utilize workflow automation tools such as Zapier, Integromat, or Microsoft Power Automate to connect different apps and automate routine tasks. These tools enable seamless integration between platforms, streamline processes, and save time.

3. **Adopt marketing automation software**: Implement marketing automation software like HubSpot, Mailchimp, or ActiveCampaign to automate email campaigns, lead nurturing, and customer segmentation.

These tools help enhance customer engagement, track performance, and optimize marketing efforts.

4. **Invest in customer service automation**: Deploy chatbots or AI-powered tools to automate customer service inquiries, provide instant responses, and streamline support processes. Automated customer service solutions can improve response times and enhance the overall customer experience.

CONCLUSION

By implementing strategic approaches such as leveraging outsourcing, embracing automation, carefully evaluating and improving processes, and prioritizing sustainability, a 0 Risk Startup-Business can thrive and succeed in the competitive business landscape. With a focus on innovation, efficiency, and adaptability, entrepreneurs can navigate challenges with confidence and drive long-term growth without compromising on risk management. By staying proactive, agile, and committed to continuous improvement, a 0 Risk Startup-Business has the potential to achieve lasting success and make a significant impact in the market.

www.ingramcontent.com/pod-product-compliance
Lightning Source LLC
Chambersburg PA
CBHW072058230526
45479CB00010B/1129